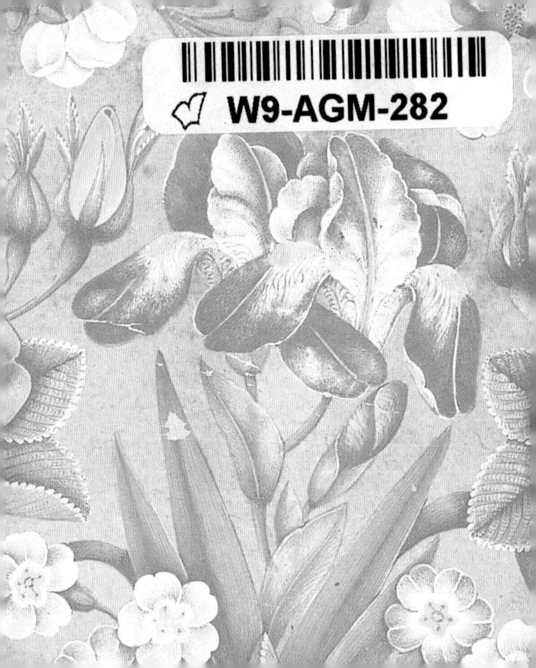

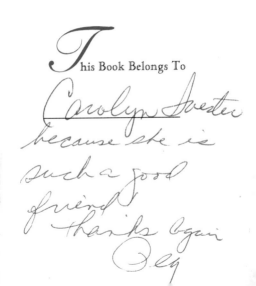

This Book Belongs To

Carolyn Sweeter
because she is
such a good
friend
thanks again
Peg

Thank You

A Book of Gratitude and Friendship

Ariel Books
Andrews and McMeel
Kansas City

THANK YOU: A BOOK OF GRATITUDE
AND FRIENDSHIP

For information write Andrews and McMeel,
a Universal Press Syndicate Company, 4900
Main Street, Kansas City, Missouri 64112.

ISBN: 0-8362-3029-9

Library of Congress Catalog Card Number:
92-73437

Thank You

T

he greatest gift of life

is friendship, and I have

received it.

HUBERT HUMPHREY

Thank You

In prosperity our friends know us; in adversity we know our friends.

9

CHURTON COLLINS

Thank You

A friend may well be reckoned the masterpiece of nature.

RALPH WALDO EMERSON

And though I ebb in worth, I'll flow in thanks.

JOHN TAYLOR

Thank You

Your bounty is beyond my speaking. But though my mouth be dumb, my heart shall thank you.

NICHOLAS ROWE

12
—

Thank You

A true friend is the most
precious of all possessions
and the one we think least
about acquiring.

François, Duc de la Rochefoucauld

riendship is a strong and habitual inclination in two persons to promote the good and happiness of one another.

14
—

EUSTACE BUDGELL

Thank You

The best portion of a good
    man's life,
His little, nameless,
    unremembered acts
Of kindness and love.

WILLIAM WORDSWORTH

17
—

A true friend unbosoms freely, advises justly, assists readily, adventures boldly, takes all patiently, defends courageously, and continues a friend unchangeably.

WILLIAM PENN

18
—

Thank You

Wherever you are it is your own friends who make your world.

WILLIAM JAMES

19
—

A sympathetic friend can be quite as dear as a brother.

HOMER

20
—

*M*y best friend is the one who brings out the best in me.

HENRY FORD

Thank You

Our chief want in life is someone who will make us do what we can.

RALPH WALDO EMERSON

21
—

Thank You

No matter what accomplishments you make, somebody helps you.

ALTHEA GIBSON

22
—

Thank You

Those who bring sunshine into the lives of others cannot keep it from themselves.

23

—

JAMES M. BARRIE

Thank You

As I think of the word "friend," I recall that all the really great things in life and all the great impelling forces are expressed in the simplest words: "God," "love," "child," "friend."

LYNDON B. JOHNSON

Thank You

I expect to pass through this world but once. Any good that I can do or any kindness that I can show to my fellow creature, let me do it now. Let me not defer or neglect it, for I shall not pass this way again.

STEPHEN GRELLET

Thank You

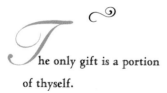

No act of kindness, no matter how small, is ever wasted.

AESOP

The only gift is a portion of thyself.

RALPH WALDO EMERSON

Life is not worth living for the man who has not even one good friend.

28

—

DEMOCRITUS OF ABDERA

Thank You

The greatest grace of a gift,

perhaps, is that it anticipates

and admits of no return.

30

HENRY WADSWORTH LONGFELLOW

Thank You

A kind heart is a fountain of gladness, making everything in its vicinity freshen into smiles. 31

WASHINGTON IRVING

Thank You

A gift, with a kind coun-
tenance, is a double present.

THOMAS FULLER

*I*t's the friends you can call
up at 4:00 A.M. that matter.

MARLENE DIETRICH

Thank You

Kind hearts are the garden,

Kind thoughts are the roots,

Kind words are the blossoms, 35

Kind deeds are the fruit.

JOHN RUSKIN

Thank You

Kind words can be short and
easy to speak, but their echoes
are endless.

37
—

MOTHER TERESA

Thank You

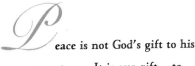

eace is not God's gift to his
creatures. It is our gift—to
each other.

38

ELIE WIESEL

Thank You

*L*ittle words of kindness,

    little words of love,

Make this earth an Eden,

    like the heaven above.

Julia Carney, "Little Things"

Thank You

So many gods, so many creeds,

So many paths that wind and wind,

40 While just the art of being kind,

— Is all this sad world needs.

ELLA WHEELER WILCOX,

"THE WORLD'S NEED"

Thank You

One of life's gifts is that each of us, no matter how tired and downtrodden, finds

reasons for thankfulness.

J. ROBERT MOSKIN

Thank You

I feel a very unusual sensation. It is not indigestion; I think it must be gratitude.

BENJAMIN DISRAELI

Thank You

Thanksgiving comes to us out
of prehistoric dimness, universal
to all ages and faiths. At
whatever straws we may grasp,
there is always a new time for
gratitude and new beginnings.

J. ROBERT MOSKIN

43
—

Thank You

Think where man's glory

begins and ends,

44

And my glory was I had such

friends.

WILLIAM BUTLER YEATS

Thank You

Greater love hath no man than this, that a man lay down his life for his friends.

45
—

JOHN 15:13

Chance makes our parents,

but choice makes our friends.

JACQUES DELILLE

46

—

Good friends are good for

your health.

IRWIN SARASON

Thank You

*H*appy is the man who finds a generous friend.

GREEK PROVERB

*F*riendships multiply joys, and divide grief.

THOMAS FULLER

Thank You

My best friend is the man who in wishing me well does so for my own sake.

ARISTOTLE

Thank You

Your friend is the man who knows all about you and still likes you.

ELBERT HUBBARD

Thank You

She became for me an island
of light, fun, and wisdom
where I could run with my
discoveries and torments and
hopes at any time of the day
and find welcome.

MAY SARTON

Thank You

In prosperity a pleasure, a solace in adversity, in grief a comfort, in joy a merry companion, at all times an other I.

JOHN LYLY

We wander through this life together in a semi-darkness in which none of us can distinguish exactly the features of his neighbor. Only from time to time, through some experience that we have of our companion,

or through some remark that
he passes, he stands for a
moment close to us, as
though illuminated by
a flash of lightning. Then we
see him as he really is.

ALBERT SCHWEITZER

55
—

Thank You

A hundred times a day I remind myself that my inner and outer life depends on the labors of other men, living and dead, and that I must exert myself to give in the same measure as I have received.

ALBERT EINSTEIN

Thank You

May I forget
What ought to be forgotten;
  and recall
Unfailingly, all
That ought to be recalled,
  each kindly thing,
Forgetting what might sting.

MATY CAROLINE DAVIES

Thank You

The supreme happiness of life
is the conviction of being loved
for yourself, or, more
correctly, in spite of yourself.

VICTOR HUGO

Thank You

Life is mostly froth and
    bubble,
60
Two things stand like stone,
Kindness in another's
    trouble,
Courage in your own.

ADAM LINDSAY GORDON,

"YE WEARIE WAYFARER"

Thank You

*N*o love, no friendship can cross the path of our destiny without leaving some mark on it forever.

FRANÇOIS MAURIAC

Thank You

T like not only to be loved,
but to be told that I am loved;
the realm of silence is large
enough beyond the grave.

GEORGE ELIOT

Thank You

*I*t's not so much our friends'
help that helps us as the
confidence that they will
help us.

EPICURUS

Thank You

So long as we are loved by others, I would almost say that

we are indispensable; and no man is useless while he has a friend.

Robert Louis Stevenson

Thank You

What is so pleasant as these jets of affection which make a young world for me again?

RALPH WALDO EMERSON

Thank You

The making of friends who are
real friends, is the best token we
have of a man's success in life.   69

———

EDWARD EVERETT HALE

Thank You

I no doubt deserved my enemies, but I don't believe I deserved my friends.

WALT WHITMAN

Thank You

*W*ithout friends no one would choose to live, though he had all other goods.

75

ARISTOTLE

*F*riendship is a single soul
dwelling in two bodies.

EURIPIDES

*T*oo much of a good thing is
wonderful.

LIBERACE

Thank You

We want but two or three friends, but these we cannot do without, and they serve us in every thought we think.

RALPH WALDO EMERSON

Thank You

A faithful friend is a strong
defense: and he that hath found
one hath found a treasure.

ECCLESIASTES 6:14

Thank You

Gratitude is when memory is stored in the heart and not in the mind.

Sam N. Hampton

The text of this book was set
in Cloister Openface, and the
initial caps were set in Snell
by Dix Type Inc., Syracuse,
New York.

Design by Diane Stevenson/
Snap-Haus Graphics